Pearson

Year **5**

Handwriting
Activity Workbook

Sealife

Home learning from the experts

Author:
Sarah Loader

About this book

This book supports the practice and consolidation of handwriting skills, with lots of engaging, fun activities to help children grow in confidence and ability.

Clear, consistent, cursive handwriting is not only a statutory requirement of the English curriculum, but is the gateway to success in all subjects. The ability to present ideas legibly and clearly is a critical life skill.

Handwriting made clear

- Handwriting requires strong fine-motor skills and pencil control. The tasks in this activity book develop and refine those skills.
- Key skills are learned and reinforced through a wide range of tasks to keep children engaged and interested in each activity.
- Helpful tips and reminders support children as they work.

How to use this book

- Little-and-often is a productive approach to handwriting, as handwriting requires great concentration and can be frustrating. Children can work through just one or two activities in a sitting, and stop when they lose interest to avoid it becoming negative.
- Try to complete the activities in the given order, as they progress in challenge and expectation.
- Your child will ideally work through activities independently, but it's worth being there for when support is needed.
- Explore the Progress Points with your child as they work through the book to see where further support is needed.

Getting started

- Make your child's learning space interesting and fun.
- Encourage your child to step away from any technology or energetic games a little while beforehand, and to take some deep breaths to help them focus.
- Make sure your child is holding their pencil properly.
- Sit with your child to start with, even if you're occupied with your own task.

Challenges to overcome

Writing more quickly, but with a consistently neat presentation

As children progress into upper Key Stage 2 they are expected to write much more quickly, without compromising the appearance of their handwriting. It can be useful to set small timed exercises and challenges to practise this.

Knowing which letters to join and which not to join

Children's handwriting should be consistently cursive by this stage. Feeling confident about which letters to join, and where, is a key part of developing pace in their writing, so it may be useful to remind them to think about this.

Get creative

- Encourage children to use some of the trickier spellings in this book in a piece of writing, for example 'cious' (precious, suspicious), 'cial' (special, official) and 'tial' (partial, initial).
- Children could write a description or summary of a particular event that happened in a book they have read.
- Encourage children to write a 'sales pitch' to promote their favourite TV programme, using headings and other features to organise their text.
- Children could research and write about somewhere in the world, using some of the organisational features they have practised.

English curriculum coverage

As children progress into upper Key Stage 2, there is only one key handwriting objective. Therefore as well as covering this statutory requirement, this activity book incorporates a wider range of English curriculum topics, so that the practice is meaningful and relevant. Some objectives are taken from the previous year as useful revision.

Topic	Curriculum relevance
Homophones	English Appendix 1: Spelling (Years 5 and 6)
Prefixes	English Appendix 1: Spelling (Years 3 and 4)
Spellings ending: –cious, –cial, –tial	English Appendix 1: Spelling (Years 5 and 6)
Brackets	Writing – Vocabulary, grammar and punctuation (Years 5 and 6)
Challenging vocabulary	English Appendix 1: Word list (Years 5 and 6)
Adverbials	English Appendix 2: Vocabulary, grammar and punctuation (Year 5 detail)
Endings: –able, –ably, –ant, –ancy, –ance, –ent, –ency, –ence	English Appendix 1: Word list (Years 5 and 6)
Converting nouns or adjectives into verbs using suffixes	English Appendix 2: Vocabulary, grammar and punctuation (Year 5 detail)
Writing narratives	Writing – Composition (Years 5 and 6)
Further organisation and presentational devices	Writing – Composition (Years 5 and 6)

Activity 1

Write out the sentences, choosing the correct homophones to complete each one.

herd / heard   allowed / aloud
guessed / guest   farther / father

Homophones sound the same, but mean different things. They are spelled differently.

1. You could never have [?] who the [?] of honour was!

_____

2. We all [?] the racket the [?] of cows made.

_____

3. The [?] the train moved, the smaller my [?] looked.

_____

4. No one is [?] to talk [?] in the library.

_____

Activity 2

Write a sentence of your own for one homophone in each pair.

1. _____

2. _____

3. _____

4. _____

Activity 3

Write these words out adding the correct prefix from the box for each one.

These add-ons at the beginnings of words are called prefixes.

| in   un   im   ir   sub   super   inter   anti   auto |

happy   _____

correct   _____

possible   _____

heading   _____

responsible   _____

market   _____

clockwise   _____

graph   _____

national   _____

Activity 4

Rewrite the sentences neatly, choosing a word from the box to complete each one.

Try to keep your handwriting neat and consistent.

precious   delicious   conscious   gracious   ferocious   malicious

1. It was [?] of Poppy to be so hurtful.

_____

2. Greg was not [?] of doing anything wrong.

_____

3. Dad makes [?] lunches.

_____

4. Clara was [?] about the present she was given.

_____

5. The wolf bared its teeth and gave a [?] snarl.

_____

6. This lovely old photo is [?] to me.

_____

Activity 5

Write a sentence of your own using one of the words in the box.

_____

_____

Activity 6

> Write out each word adding the suffix 'ly', and then write a sentence of your own for each word.

1. ferocious   *ferociously*
   The crocodile snapped its jaws ferociously.

2. gracious   _____
   _____

3. malicious   _____
   _____

4. conscious   _____
   _____

5. delicious   _____
   _____

6. precious   _____
   _____

❶ I can write words with –cious spellings.

Activity 7

Only the opening bracket has been included every time brackets are used in this text. Rewrite it in your best handwriting, adding the closing bracket for each pair where you think it fits best.

Brackets are used to add an explanation or aside to a sentence that is not essential to meaning.

The Dive

Jasmine climbed the ladder and watched out of the corner of her eye as the pool down below got smaller. She asked herself (not for the first time why she was doing this, why she was putting herself through such agony. But she knew (or hoped that it would be worth it.

She got to the diving board and rubbed her hands together to stop them shaking (they always shook up here and looked down at her feet. How many times had she done this?

She looked straight ahead at the clock on the far side of the pool and began counting (another ritual, then she walked forwards, curled her toes over the edge of the board and lifted her arms up, blocking out the noise (not that she could hear anything from here, and then bent her knees and took off. It was the feeling she waited for, when all the training felt worthwhile (though the score was anyone's guess.

The Dive

_____

_____

_____

_____

_____

_____

_____

_____

_____

_____

_____

_____

_____

_____

_____

_____

Activity 8

Write out the sentences, choosing the correct homophone to complete each one.

draught / draft   isle / aisle
stationary / stationery   profit / prophet

1. We go to the ? of Wight every year.

_____

2. The message from the ? was remarkable.

_____

3. There's a cold ? in the kitchen.

_____

4. The train has been ? for ages.

_____

Activity 9

Write a sentence of your own for one homophone in each pair.

1. _____

2. _____

3. _____

4. _____

2 I can write homophones.

Activity 10

Rewrite the sentences neatly, choosing a word from the box to complete each one.

Try to keep your handwriting neat and consistent.

bargain   accommodate   cemetery
definite   embarrasses   familiar

1. They couldn't ? everyone.

_____

2. The ? is peaceful and quiet.

_____

3. Nan always wore the same ? coat.

_____

4. Dad really ? me at the school gates.

_____

5. Jess loves finding a ? at the market.

_____

6. It was ? that the train had gone.

_____

Activity 11

Write a sentence of your own using one of the words in the box.

_____

_____

3 I can write challenging words.

Activity 12

> The brackets in this job advert are mixed up. Rewrite it in your best handwriting, putting the brackets in the right places.

WAITING STAFF NEEDED

The restaurant is looking for (waiting staff) for mainly weekend shifts, primarily on Saturday nights. Applicants need to be good with people, polite and (calm under pressure) the restaurant gets very busy.

Previous waiting experience is not essential, but might be useful, (so please include references) contact details below.

The applicant will be joining a tight-knit team, so needs to work (well) with others of all ages and be a good communicator.

Contact the manager with any questions or to apply (via) phone 01824 665 667, or (email) mia_the manager@TheBarn.co.uk.

WAITING STAFF NEEDED

_____

_____

_____

_____

_____

_____

_____

_____

_____

_____

_____

_____

_____

4 *I can use brackets in my writing.*

Activity 13

Rewrite the sentences neatly, choosing a word from the box to complete each one.

official   special   artificial   essential   confidential   partial

1. Last night there was a ❓ eclipse.

_____

2. There was a huge party at the ❓ opening.

_____

3. Angus is a really ❓ person.

_____

4. It was ❓ that Bryony got there on time.

_____

5. The coin looked real, but I knew it was ❓ .

_____

6. Kate knew the documents were highly ❓ .

_____

Activity 14

Write a sentence of your own using one of the words in the box.

_____

_____

Activity 15

Write out each word adding the suffix 'ly', and then write a sentence of your own for each word.

1. official   _____

_____

2. special   _____

_____

3. artificial   _____

_____

4. essential   _____

_____

5. confidential   _____

_____

6. partial   _____

_____

5 I can write words with –cial and –tial spellings.

Activity 16

The adverbial word or phrase is underlined in these sentences. Write out each sentence alongside the name of the adverbial it contains.

1. We're <u>often</u> allowed to stay up late.
2. I'm <u>definitely</u> coming this weekend.
3. I went to bed <u>happily</u>.
4. A phone rang <u>nearby</u>.
5. <u>Before long</u> they came to a bridge.
6. <u>As a result</u> of my goal we won!

(Time) _____

(Place) _____

(Manner) _____

(Frequency) _____

(Cause) _____

(Probability) _____

Activity 17

Write out the sentences from Activity 16, choosing a different adverbial word or phrase for each category.

Try to keep your handwriting neat and consistent.

| Time | soon   immediately   later   the next day |

Later, they came to a bridge.

| Place | on the ground   inside   over by   down |

| Manner | gently   slowly   energetically   enthusiastically |

| Frequency | occasionally   never   usually   always |

| Cause | therefore   so that   because   however |

| Probability | probably   maybe   possibly   surely |

Activity 18

Choose a different word from the box to complete each sentence.

tolerable adorable enjoyable changeable comfortably
understandably applicable considerably

1. The new kittens were utterly ? .

   _____

2. His experience wasn't ? to his new job.

   _____

3. It was ? colder on the mountain.

   _____

4. The weather in Scotland is so ? .

   _____

5. ? he's been very upset since the accident.

   _____

6. The teacher ensured we were sitting ? .

   _____

7. School is ? , apart from when we have maths!

   _____

8. PE is my most ? subject.

   _____

Activity 19

Write a sentence of your own for each of the words in the box from Activity 18.

Try to keep your handwriting neat and consistent.

1. _____

_____

2. _____

_____

3. _____

_____

4. _____

_____

5. _____

_____

6. _____

_____

7. _____

_____

8. _____

_____

6 I can write words with −able and −ably endings.

Activity 20

Use this plan to start a story about a sailing adventure. Remember to use paragraphs and keep your handwriting neat.

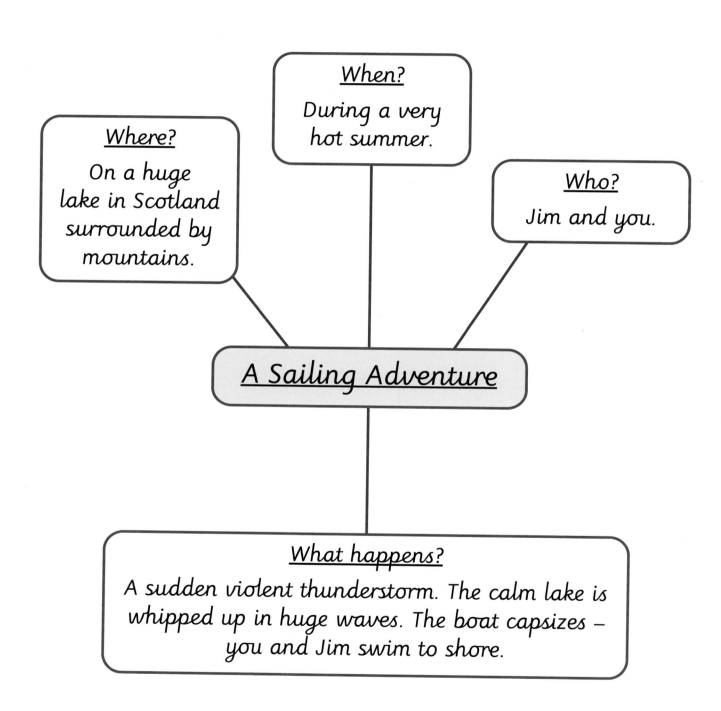

When?
During a very hot summer.

Where?
On a huge lake in Scotland surrounded by mountains.

Who?
Jim and you.

A Sailing Adventure

What happens?
A sudden violent thunderstorm. The calm lake is whipped up in huge waves. The boat capsizes – you and Jim swim to shore.

<u>A Sailing Adventure</u>

_____

_____

_____

_____

_____

_____

_____

_____

_____

_____

_____

_____

_____

_____

_____

_____

_____

_____

Activity 21

Convert these words into verbs using one of these suffixes.
You might need to take away the last letter of the root word.

ate   ise   ify

liquid   <u>liquidise</u>

equal   _____

active   _____

mummy   _____

fertile   _____

energy   _____

sign   _____

vaccine   _____

pure   _____

apology   _____

note   _____

motive   _____

Activity 22

Write a sentence of your own for each of the verbs you created in Activity 21.

Try to keep your handwriting neat and consistent.

1. _We used a blender to liquidise the fruit and yoghurt._

2. _____

3. _____

4. _____

5. _____

6. _____

7. _____

8. _____

9. _____

10. _____

11. _____

12. _____

Activity 23

Create a story plan and then start your own story. Choose one of the titles in the box or one of your own. Remember to use paragraphs and keep your handwriting neat.

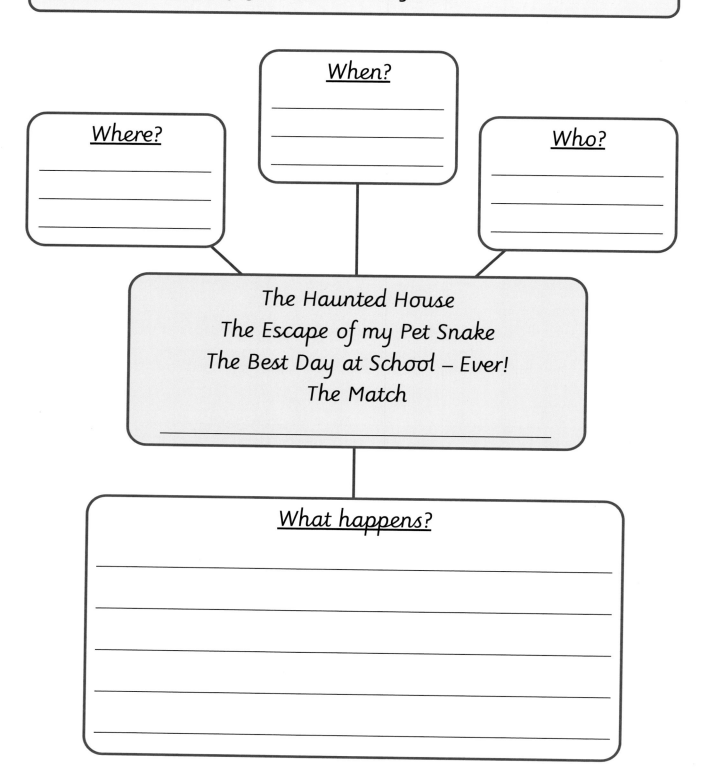

When?

Where?

Who?

The Haunted House
The Escape of my Pet Snake
The Best Day at School – Ever!
The Match

What happens?

Title: _____

_____

_____

_____

_____

_____

_____

_____

_____

_____

_____

_____

_____

_____

_____

_____

_____

7 I can plan and write my own story.

Activity 24

Choose a different word from the box to complete each sentence.

frequency hesitancy observant substance obedient
expectant innocent tolerance

1. Gran had sharp eyes and was very ? .

_____

2. The ? mothers all filed into the surgery.

_____

3. There was a slight ? in her voice.

_____

4. There was a nasty ? in Jen's bag.

_____

5. The coach had no ? for bad behaviour.

_____

6. Since his dog training, Lucky had become very ? .

_____

7. The trains go from here with great ? .

_____

8. He walked away from the mess, trying to look ? .

_____

Activity 25

Write a sentence of your own for each of the words in the box from Activity 24.

1. _____

_____

2. _____

_____

3. _____

_____

4. _____

_____

5. _____

_____

6. _____

_____

7. _____

_____

8. _____

_____

8 I can write words with –ant, –ance, –ancy, –ent and –ency endings.

Activity 26

Try to keep your handwriting neat and consistent.

Rewrite this page from a travel brochure, adding in punctuation, capital letters, paragraph breaks, sub-headings and brackets where they will help with the meaning.

The Himalayas

The Himalayas are found in South Asia and stretch 2400 kilometres 1500 miles between India Nepal and China though most of the mountain range is in India the Himalayan climate is cold and the mountain summits are covered in snow Himalaya actually means a place of snow and the snow on the summit never melts not even in high summer there are 30 mountains in total nine of which are the highest peaks in the world including the world's highest mountain Mount Everest which is 8848 metres 29029 feet above sea level the Himalayas are home to lots of plant and animal species including snow leopards, black bears, lynxes and red foxes so there's a huge amount to see that is unique to the region and the trekking is spectacular.

The Himalayas

_____

_____

_____

_____

_____

_____

_____

_____

_____

_____

_____

_____

_____

_____

_____

_____

9 I can write neatly, fluently and quickly.

Activity 27

Choose a different word from the box to complete each sentence.

confident hesitant frequent independence emergency
assistance decency tolerant

1. Laura was ? , even before she won gold.

_____

2. The ? exit has a green sign.

_____

3. I am allowed more ? than my little sister.

_____

4. My family made ? trips to London.

_____

5. I needed Aaron's ? to move the boxes.

_____

6. Jamil is ? of his brother's annoying music.

_____

7. Mum was ? about letting me stay out.

_____

8. Basic ? is expected of everyone.

_____

Activity 28

Write a sentence of your own for each of the words in the box in Activity 27.

1. _____

   _____

2. _____

   _____

3. _____

   _____

4. _____

   _____

5. _____

   _____

6. _____

   _____

7. _____

   _____

8. _____

   _____

10 I can write words with –ant, –ance, –ent, –ence and –ency endings.

My name is _____